CLASSIC ROMAN ALPHABETS

100 COMPLETE FONTS

SELECTED AND ARRANGED BY
DAN X. SOLO
FROM THE SOLOTYPE
TYPOGRAPHERS CATALOG

DOVER PUBLICATIONS, INC., NEW YORK

Published in Canada by General Publishing Company, Ltd., 30 Lesmill Road, Don Mills, Toronto, Ontario.

Published in the United Kingdom by Constable and Company, Ltd., 10 Orange Street, London WC2H 7EG.

Classic Roman Alphabets: 100 Complete Fonts is a new work, first published by Dover Publications, Inc., in 1983.

DOVER *Pictorial Archive* SERIES

Classic Roman Alphabets: 100 Complete Fonts is a title in the Dover Pictorial Archive Series. Up to six words may be composed from the letters in these alphabets and used in any single publication without payment to or permission from the publisher. For any more extensive use, write directly to Solotype Typographers, 298 Crestmont Drive, Oakland, California 94619, who have the facilities to typeset extensively in varying sizes and according to specifications. The republication of this book as a whole is prohibited.

Manufactured in the United States of America
Dover Publications, Inc., 180 Varick Street, New York, N.Y. 10014

Library of Congress Cataloging in Publication Data
Main entry under title:

Classic roman alphabets.

(Dover pictorial archive series)
1. Type and type-founding—Roman type. 2. Printing—Specimens. 3. Alphabets.
I. Solo, Dan X.   II. Solotype Typographers.   III. Series.
Z250.5.R64C57   1983   686.2′24   83-5235
ISBN 0-486-24517-9

Albertus

ABCDEFG
HIJKLMMMNOPQR
STUVWWXYZ

abcdefghijklm
nopqrstuvwxyz

1234567890

([&&$$¢.,:;"--!?])

Americana

ABCDEFGH
IJKLMNOPQRS
TUVWXYŶZ

abcdefghijklm
nopqrstuvwxyz

1234567890

(&$$$¢¢⁄∴;''!?⸮-·*)

Aster

ABCDEFG HIJKLMNOPQ RSTUVWXYZ

abcdefghijklm nopqrstuvwxyz

1234567890 (&$¢/.,:;?!-""''*)

Aster Italic

ABCDEFG
HIJKLMNOPQR
STUVWXYZ

abcdefghijklm
nopqrstuvwxyz,

1234567890
(&$¢/.,.:;?!-'''""'*)

Baskerville

ABCDEFG
HIJKLMNOPQRS
TUVWXYZ

abcdefghijklm
nopqrstuvwxyz

1234567890

(&$¢$¢%;,!?"-*)

Bauer Bodoni

ABCDEFGHI
JKLMNOPQRS
TUVWXYZ
abcdefghijklmno
pqrstuvwxyz

1234567890
(&:;-'""!?$£)

Bauer Bodoni Italic

ABCDEFGHI
JKLMNOPQRS
TUVWXYZ
abcdefghijklmno
pqrstuvwxyz

1234567890
(&:;-'"''!?$£)

Bembo

ABCDEFGHI
JKLMNOPQRS
TUVWXYZ

abcdefghijklmno
pqrstuvwxyz

1234567890
(&.,.:;""""!?)

Bembo Italic

ABCDEFGHI
JKLMNOPQRS
TUVWXYZ

abcdefghijklmnop
qrstuvwxyz

1234567890
&.,:;'‛‛"!?

Benedictine Book

ABCDEFGH
IJKLMNOPQR
STUVWXYZ

abcdefghijklm
nopqrstuvwxyz

1234567890
(&:;-'"!?$)

Berling Roman

ABCDEFGHI
JKLMNOPQRS
TUVWXYZ

abcdefghijklmnop
qrstuvwxyz

1234567890

(&.,''""‚'!?)

Berling Italic

ABCDEFGHI
JKLMNOPQRS
TUVWXYZ

abcdefghijklmnop
qrstuvwxyz

1234567890
(&.,'""!?)

Bernhard Modern Roman

ABCDEFGHI
JKLMNOPQRS
TUVWXYZ

abcdefghijklmnop
qrstuvwxyz

1234567890
&.,.;!?'"""-$¢

Bernhard Modern Italic

ABCDEFGHI
JKLMNOPQRS
TUVWXYZ

abcdefghijklmnop
qrstuvwxyz

1234567890
&.,.;:!?""""-Th$

Bodoni

ABCDEFGHIJKLM
NOPQRSTUVWXYZ

abcdefghijklm
nopqrstuvwxyz

1234567890

(&$¢/.,.:;!?""-*)

Bodoni Italic

ABCDEFGHIJKLM
NOPQRSTUVWXYZ

abcdefghijklm
nopqrstuvvuwxyz

1234567890

(&$¢%,.:;!?-‘’*)

Bookman

ABCDEFGHI
JKLMNOPQR
STUVWXYZ
abcdefghijklmn
opqrstuvwxyz

12345 & 67890

(&.:;-"!?£$ of The)

A M R ry

Bulmer

ABCDEFGHIJKLM
NOPQRSTUVWXYZ

abcdefghijklm
nopqrstuvwxyz

1234567890

(&$¢$¢%.,.;!?'""-_*)

Bulmer Italic

ABCDEF*J*GHIJKLM
NOPQRSTUVWXYZ

abcdefghijklm
nopqrstuvwxyz fffl ffflffl

1234567890

(&$$¢¢%.,.:;'"""!?--*)

Caledonia

ABCDEFG HIJKLMNOPQR STUVWXYZ

abcdefgghijklmno ppqqrstuvwxyyz

1234567890

(&$¢%⁄,.:,!?''-*)

Caledonia Italic

ABCDEFG HIJKLMNOPQR STUVWXYZ

abcdefghijklm nopqrstuvwxyz

1234567890

(&$¢/.,.;''!?-*)

Caledonia Bold

ABCDEFG
HIJKLMNOPQR
STUVWXYZ

abcdefghijklm
nopqrstuvwxyz

1234567890

(&$¢%.,:;!?'""-*)

Caslon Shaded

ABCDEFGHI
JKLMNOPQRS
TUVWXYZ

abcdefghijklmno
pqrstuvwxyz

1234567890
(&.,;:"''"''-!?)

Caslon No. 540

ABCDEFG
HIJKLMNOPQR
STUVWXYZ

abcdefghijklmnop
qrstuvwxyz

1234567890

(&$!?¢%/*)

Caslon No.540 Italic

ABCDEFG
HIJKLMNOPQR
STUVWXYZ

abcdefghijklmnopqr
stuvwxyz

1234567890

(&$£.!?¢%//*)

Centaur

ABCDEFG
HIJKLMNOPQRS
TUVWXYZ

abcdefghijklm
nopqrstuvwxyz

1234567890

(&$/.,.:;"'!?[]-^ˇ˜°¨¿¡+®*)

Centaur Italic

ABCDEFG
HIJKLMNOPQRS
TUVWXYZ

abcdefghijklm
nopqrstuvwxyz

1234567890

(&$s¢/:;'‘’!?-*)

Century Expanded

ABCDEFGHIJKLM
NOPQRSTUVWXYZ

abcdefghijklm
nopqrstuvwxyz

1234567890

(&$¢$%,.:;!?"-*)

Century Expanded Italic

ABCDEFGHIJKLM
NOPQRSTUVWXYZ

abcdefghijklm
nopqrstuvwxyz

1234567890

(&$¢$%.,.;''-?!*)

Century Schoolbook

ABCDEFGHIJKLM NOPQRSTUVWXYZ

abcdefghijklm nopqrstuvwxyz

1234567890

(&$$%.,.;!?""''-'*)

Century Schoolbook Italic

ABCDEFGHIJKLM
NOPQRSTUVWXYZ

abcdeffiflghijklm
nopqrstuvwxyz

1234567890

(&$¢$¢%.,.:;!?'"-*)

Cheltenham Medium

ABCDEFG
HIJKLMNOPQR
STUVWXYZ

abcdefghijklm
nopqrstuvwxyz

1234567890

(&$$¢/.,:;"'!?-©®*)

Cheltenham Medium Italic

ABCDEFG
HIJKLMNOPQRS
TUVWXYZ

abcdefghijklm
nopqrstuvwxyz

1234567890

(&$¢/.,.;""!?-*)

Clearface Bold

ABCDEFG
HIJKLMNOPQR
STUVWXYZ

abcdefghijklmnop
qrstuvwxyz

1234567890

(&&&$$£!?¢%)

Cloister Old Style

ABCDEFGHI
JKLMNOPQQR
STUVWXYZ
abcdefghijklmno
pqrstuvwxyz

1234567890
(&.,:;'"-!?)

Cloister Bold

ABCDEFG
HIJKLMNOPQR
STUVWXYZ

abcctdefghijklm
nopqrstuvwxyz

1234567890

(&$¢/.,:;-'"!?*)

Cochin Old Style

ABCDEFGHI
JKLMNOPQRS
TUVWXYZ

abcdefghijklmno
pqrstuvwxyz

1234567890
(&:;-'!?$£)

Colwell Handletter

ABCDEFGHI
JKLMNOPQRS
TUVWXYZ

abcdefghijklmno
pqrstuvwxyz

1234567890
&:;-'"!?$

Cooper Old Style

ABCDEFGHI
JKLMNOPQRS
TUVWXYZ

abcdefghijklmnop
qrstuvwxyz

1234567890
{&:;-'"!?$}

Cooper Old Style Italic

ABCDEFGHI
JKLMNOPQRS
TUVWXYZ

abcdefghijklmnop
qrstuvwxyz

1234567890
(&:;-'"!?$)

Deepdene

ABCDEFGHI
JKLMNOPQRS
TUVWXYZ

abcdefghijklmno
pqrstuvwxyz

1234567890

(&.:;-'"!?$)

Della Robbia

ABCDEFGHI
JKLMNOPQRS
TUVWXYZ

abcdefghijklmno
pqrstuvwxyz

1234567890
&:;,-"!?$

Dominante

ABCDEFG
HIJKLMNOPQR
STUVWXYZ

abcdefghijklm
nopqrstuvwxyz

1234567890

&$.,.:;!?

Dominante Italic

ABCDEFG
HIJKLMNOPQR
STUVWXYZ

abcdefghijklm
nopqrstuvwxyz

1234567890

&$.,:;!?

Egmont

ABCDEFGHIJ
KLMNOPQRS
TUVWXYZ

abcdefghijklmnop
qrstuvwxyz

1234567890
&.,:;?!'()-$

Egmont Bold

ABCDEFGHIJ
KLMNOPQRS
TUVWXYZ

abcdefghijklmnop
qrstuvwxyz

1234567890
&.,:;?!'()-$

ENGRAVERS ROMAN

ABCDEF
GHIJKLM
NOPQRST
UVWXYZ

1234567890

(&$%/.:.,;-""'!?*)

ERICUS

ABCDEF
GHIJKLM
NOPQR
STUVW
XYZ

Eve Light

ABCDEFG
HIJKLMNOPQRS
TUVWXYZ

abcdefghijklm
nopqrstuvwxyz

1234567890

(&:;="!?$.:-+ᵽ)

Eve Heavy

ABCDEFG
HIJKLMNOPQRS
TUVWXYZ

abcdefghijklm
nopqrstuvwxyz

1234567890

(&$$$¢/.,:;="'!?❖-+-)

Firmin Didot

ABCDEFG HIJKLMNOPQR STUVWXYZ

abcdefghijklm nopqrstuvwxyz

1234567890

(&$$¢¢%/.,:;''""!?-·[]*)

Friz Quadrata

ABCDEFG
HIJKLMNOPQR
STUUVWXYZ

abcdefghijklm
nopqrstuvwxyz

1234567890
1234567890
(&$¢//.,:;"""''''''!?-*)

Garamond Old Style

ABCDEFGHIJKLM
NOPQRSTUVWXYZ

abcdefghijklm
nopqrstuvwxyz

1234567890

(&$¢/.,:;'"!?-*)

Garamond Old Style Italic

ABCDEFGHIJKLM
NOPQRSTUVWXYZ

abcdefghijklm
nopqrstuvwxyz

1234567890

(&$¢&/.,.;:!?""-*)

Garamond Bold

ABCDEFG
HIJKLMNOPQR
STUVWXYZ

abcdefghijklm
nopqrstuvwxyz

1234567890
(&$¢.,;:!?%/'"'")

Goudy Old Style

ABCDEFG
HIJKLMNOPQR
STUVWXYZ

abcdefghijklm
nopqrstuvwxyz

1234567890

(&$$¢¢%.,.;""!?-–·*)

Goudy Old Style Italic

ABCDEFGHIJKLM
NOPQRSTUVWXYYZ
abcdefghijklm
nopqrstuvwxyz
1234567890
&℘,.;:-'"!?$¢

AABCDEFG
HIJKLMNNOPQ
RSTTUUWXYZ
egm_n_t_vw

Grasset Roman

ABCDEFGHI
JKLMNOPQR
STUVWXYZ

abcdefghijklmno
pqrstuvwxyz

1234567890
(&.:;-'"!?)

Grasset Italic

AABCDEFGHI
JKLMNOPQR
STUVWXYZ

abcdefghijklmno
pqrstuvwxyz

1234567890
.,;-'"!?&

Hess Oldstyle

ABCDEFGHI
JKLMNOPQR
STUVWXYZ

abcdefghijklmn
opqrstuvwxyz

1234567890
(&:;-''!?$)

Hess Penletter

AABCDEFGH
IJKLMNOPQR
STUVWXYZ

abcdeefghijklmnop
qrstuvwxyz

$1234567890
& .,:;-'"!?

Horley Old Face

ABCDEFGHI JKLMNOPQRS TUVWXYZ

abcdefghijklmno pqrstuvwxyz

1234567890 &.,:;!?-""

Joanna

ABCDEFGHI
JKLMNOPQRS
TUVWXYZ

abcdefghijklmn
opqrstuvwxyz

1234567890
&.,.:,-'!?()

Melior

ABCDEFGHIJKLM
NOPQRSTUVWXYZ

abcdefghijklm
nopqrstuvwxyz

1234567890

(&$¢/.,.:;!?"-*)

Melior Italic

ABCDEFGHIJKLM
NOPQRSTUVWXYZ

abcdefghijklm
nopqrstuvwxyz

1234567890

(&$¢%,.:;''!?-·*)

Meridien Light

ABCDEFGHI
JKLMNOPQRS
TUVWXYZ

abcdefghijklmno
pqrstuvwxyz

1234567890
(&.,:;'-"" !?)

MICHELANGELO

A
BCD
EFGHI
JKLMNO
PQRSTUVW
XYZ

1234567890

Minster Medium

ABCDEFGHI
JKLMNOPQRS
TUVWXYZ

abcdefghijklmnop
qrstuvwxyz

1234567890
(&.,„.;;–""!?)

Modern No. 20

ABCDEFGHI
JKLMNOPQR
STUVWXYZ

abcdefghijklmn
opqrstuvwxyz

1234567890

(&.,.:;"""-£)

Nicholas Cochin

ABCDEFGHI
JKLMNOPQR
STUVWXYZ

abcdefghijklmnop
qrstuvwxyz

1234567890
&:;?$

Nicholas Cochin Italic

ABCDEFGHI
JKLMNOPQR
STUVWXYZ

abcddee fghijklmnn
opqrr stt uvwxyz

1234567890
(&.;-'!?$)

Nova Augustea

ABCDEFGHI
JKLMNOPQRS
TUVWXYZ

abcdefffghijklm
nopqrstuvwxyz

1234567890
&.,::;'""""!?

Palatino

ABCDEFG
HIJKLMNOPQ
RSTUVWXYZ

abcdefghijklm
nopqrstuvwxyz

1234567890

Qu(&$$¢¢%.,:;!?""-=*)

Palatino Italic

AABBCDDEEFFGG
HHIJJKKLLMM
NNOPPQQRRSSTT
ThUVUWWXYZZ

abcdee fghijkklm
nopqrstuvwxyz

1234567890

(&$$¢¢/.,:;?!-'""*)

Perpetua

ABCDEFG
HIJKLMNOPQRS
TUVWXYZ

abcdefghijklm
nopqrstuvwxyz

1234567890

(&$.,.:;!?"-)

Perpetua Italic

ABCDEFG
HIJKLMNOPQRS
TUVWXYZ

abcdefghijklm
nopqrstuvwxyz

1234567890

(& $.,.:;!?"-)

Plantin

ABCDEFG
HIJKLMNOPQR
STUVWXYZ

abcdefghijklm
nopqrstuvwxyz

1234567890

(&$$¢¢%,.:;-'''!?)

Plantin Italic

ABCDEFGHI
JKLMNOPQRS
TUVWXYZ

abcdefghijklmno
pqrstuvwxyz

1234567890

(&:;,!?'''''-–·$¢)

Romana Normal

ABCDEFG
HIJKLMNOPQR
STUVWXYZ

abcdefghijklm
nopqrstuvwxyz

1234567890

(&$¢/.,:;?!-"'~^··^*)

Sabon

ABCDEFGHI JKLMNOPQRS TUVWXYZ

abcdefghijklmno pqrstuvwxyz

1234567890
1234567890
&&.,:;‰§†?!()

SCHNEIDLER INITIALS

ABCDEF
GHIJKLM
NOPQR
STUVW
XYZ

SISTINA TITLING

ABCDEF
GHIJKLM
NOPQR
STUVW
XYZ

1234567890

Tiffany Light

ABCDEFG
HIJJKKLMNOPQ
RRSTUVWXYZ

abcdeefghijkklm
nopqrstuvwxyz

1234567890

(&(&$$$¢¢/.,:;""''!?–-.**)

Times Roman

ABCDEFG
HIJKLMNOPQ
RSTUVWXYZ

abcdefghijklm
nopqrstuvwxyz

1234567890

(&$¢%/.,.:;""!?-*)

Times Italic

ABCDEFG
HIJKLMNOPQ
RSTUVWXYZ

abcdefghijklm
nopqrstuvwxyz

1234567890

(&$¢%/.,.:;!?''-*)

Torino

ABCDEFGHIJKLM
NOPQRSTUVWXYZ

abcdefghijklm
nopqrstuvwxyz

1234567890

(&$$¢¢%,.:;""!?-·*)

Torino Italic

ABCDEFGHIJKLM
NOPQRSTUVWXYZ

abcdefghijklm
nopqrstuvwxyz

1234567890

(&$¢/.,'''!?)

Trajanus

ABCDEFG
HIJKLMNOPQR
STUVWXYZ

abcdefghijklm
nopqrstuvwxyz

1234567890

(&$¢.,:;!?%/"-)

Trajanus Italic

ABCDEFG
HIJKLMNOPQR
STUVWXYZ

abcdefghijklm
nopqrstuvwxyz

1234567890
(&$$¢¢%/.,:;""'"!?--*)

Trajanus Bold

ABCDEFG
HIJKLMNOPQR
STUVWXYZ

abcdefghijklm
nopqrstuvwxyz

1234567890

(&$¢.,.:;!?%/""-)

Trump Mediaeval

ABCDEFGHIJKL
MNOPQRSTUVWXYZ

abcdefghijkl
mnopqrstuvwxyz

12345 1234567890 67890

ÄÇËÈÉÊÖÜ

äàáâçëèéêïìíîöòóôüùúû

(&$£!?¢%/ *
ÆŒQuæœfffifl)

Trump Mediaeval Italic

ABCDEFGHIJKL
MNOPQRSTUVWXYZ

abcdefghijkl
mnopqrstuvwxyz

1234567890

ÄÇËÈÉÊÖÜ

äàáâçëèéêïìíîöòóôüìùúû

(&$£!?¢%æœfffifl)

Vendome

ABCDEFGHI
JKLMNOPQRS
TUVWXYZ

abcdefghijklmno
pqrstuvwxyz

1234567890
(&.,:;'‐''""!?)

Verona

ABCDEFGHI
JKLMNOPQRS
TUVWXYZ

abcdefghijklmnop
qrstuvwxyz

1234567890
&.,:;‚‚""!?()

Walbaum

ABCDEFGH
IJKLMNOPQR
STUVWXYZ
(&:;-!?''"$£)
abcdefghijklmn
opqrstuvwxyz

1234567890

Weiss Roman

ABCDEFGHI
JKLMNOPQRS
TUVWXYZ

abcdefghijklmnop
qrstuvwxyz

1234567890

WEISS INITIALS NO.1

ABCDEF
GHIJKLM
NOPQR
STUVW
XYZ

1234567890

WEISS INITIALS NO.3

ABCDEF
GHIJKLM
NOPQR
STUVW
XYZ

1234567890

Windsor Light

ABCDEFGHI
JKLMNOPQR
STUVWXYZ

abcdefghijklmno
pqrstuvwxyz

&

£1234567890
(.,"-!?)

Worcester Round

ABCDEFGH
IJKLMNOPQR
STUVWXYZ

abcdefghijklmno
pqrstuvwxyz

1234567890
(&.,:;-'!?)